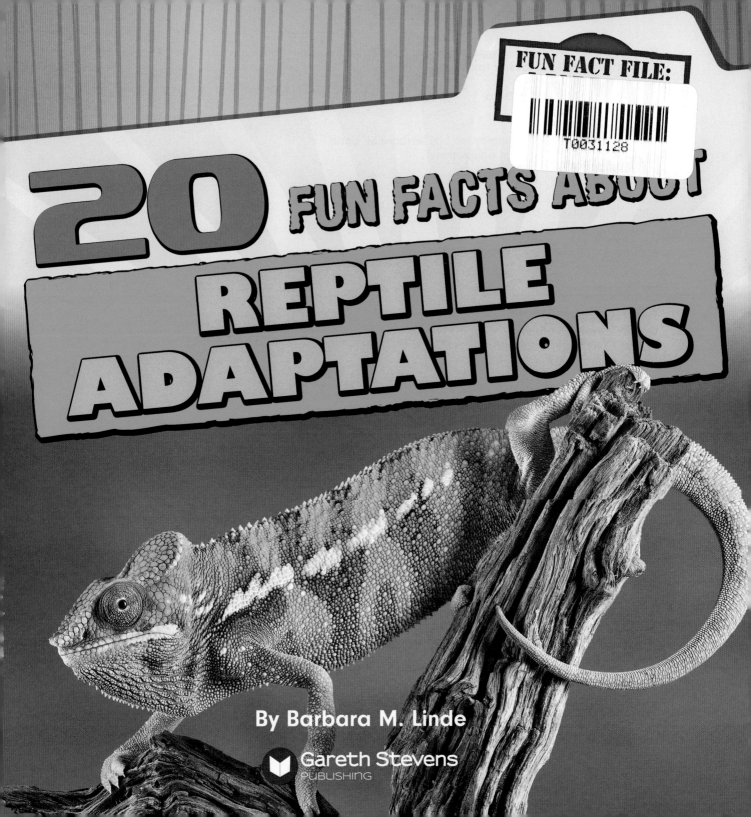

FUN FACT FILE:

T0031128

20 FUN FACTS ABOUT REPTILE ADAPTATIONS

By Barbara M. Linde

Gareth Stevens
PUBLISHING

Please visit our website, www.garethstevens.com. For a free color catalog of all our high-quality books, call toll free 1-800-542-2595 or fax 1-877-542-2596.

Cataloging-in-Publication Data

Linde, Barbara M.
20 fun facts about reptile adaptations / by Barbara M. Linde.
p. cm. — (Fun fact file: animal adaptations)
Includes index.
ISBN 978-1-4824-4452-0 (pbk.)
ISBN 978-1-4824-4396-7 (6-pack)
ISBN 978-1-4824-4434-6 (library binding)
1. Reptiles — Juvenile literature. 2. Animals — Adaptation — Juvenile literature. I. Linde, Barbara M. II. Title.
QL644.2 L56 2016
597.9—d23

First Edition

Published in 2017 by
Gareth Stevens Publishing
111 East 14th Street, Suite 349
New York, NY 10003

Copyright © 2017 Gareth Stevens Publishing

Designer: Andrea Davison-Bartolotta
Editor: Kristen Nelson

Photo credits: Cover, p. 1 Cathy Keifer/Shutterstock.com; p. 4 Irina oxilixo Danilova/Shutterstock.com; p. 5 (top left) KAMONRAT/Shutterstock.com; p. 5 (top right) davemhuntphotography/Shutterstock.com; p. 5 (middle left) worananphoto/iStock/Thinkstock; p. 5 (middle right) Sanne vd Berg Fotografie/Shutterstock.com; p. 5 (bottom left) acasali/Shutterstock.com; p. 5 (bottom right) Longjourneys/Shutterstock.com; p. 6 Sean Lema/Shutterstock.com; p. 7 Cameramannz/Shutterstock.com; p. 8 (top) Marietjie/Shutterstock.com; p. 8 (bottom) J. L. Levy/Shutterstock.com; pp. 9 (main), 10 Arto Hakola/Shutterstock.com; p. 9 (inset) Eric Isselee/Shutterstock.com; p. 11 J Fusco Paul/Getty Images; p. 12 reptiles4all/Shutterstock.com; p. 13 Cathy Keifer/iStock/Thinkstock; p. 14 Digital Vision/Getty Images; p. 15 (background texture) Ameu/Shutterstock.com; p. 16 (top) JohnPitcher/iStock/Thinkstock; p. 16 (bottom) Heiko Kiera/Shutterstock.com; p. 17 johnaudrey/iStock/Thinkstock; p. 18 JedsPics_com/iStock/Thinkstock; p. 19 DEA/C.DANI/I.JESKE/Getty Images; p. 20 jurra8/Shutterstock.com; p. 21 Richard Whitcombe/Shutterstock.com; p. 22 (bottom) Patrick K. Campbell/Shutterstock.com; pp. 22 (top), 24 Matt Jeppson/Shutterstock.com; p. 23 (top) bbb/Getty Images; p. 23 (bottom) dr322/Shutterstock.com; p. 25 James Gerholdt/Getty Images; p. 26 DEA Picture Library/Getty Images; p. 27 kerstiny/Shutterstock.com; p. 28 Richard Susanto/Shutterstock.com; p. 29 Sean Gallup/Getty Images.

Printed in the United States of America

CPSIA compliance information: Batch #CS16GS: For further information contact Gareth Stevens, New York, New York at 1-800-542-2595.

Contents

Words in the glossary appear in **bold** type the first time they are used in the text.

Remarkable Reptiles

How do you know if an animal is a reptile? Reptiles walk or **slither** on land and often swim well and spend time in water. They have hard scales covering their body, breathe air with their lungs, and lay eggs.

Millions of years ago, the **ancestors** of reptiles lived in the sea. Over time, some of them moved to land. As they did, they adapted, or changed their body and **behavior** to live better in their new **environment**. Let's find out about some of these fascinating adaptations!

These animals are all reptiles!

5

FACT 1

A reptile's body is powerless to control its temperature.

When reptiles get cold, they bask, or lay in the sun, to warm up. They move to the shade when they get too hot. They may be active only part of the day or year.

This chuckwalla basks in the desert sun and stays active in temperatures up to 102°F (39°C).

The tuatara lives only in New Zealand. It's the only animal of its kind in the world.

The tuatara tells time with its third eye.

A bump on top of the tuatara's head has eye parts in it, but it's covered with scales! It's not used for seeing like the tuatara's other eyes are. Scientists think the eye helps the tuatara know the time of day or the season of the year.

FACT 3

How often a snake sheds depends on the kind of snake, its age, and how healthy it is.

Snakes get all new skin a few times each year.

Snakes grow larger their whole life, but their skin doesn't keep growing. A new skin forms under the old one. The snake **sheds** by tearing the old skin and crawling out of it, nose first.

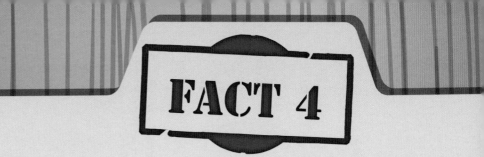
Alligators may grow as many as 3,000 teeth during their life!

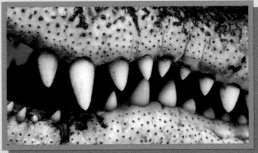

If a crocodilian's tooth falls out, a new tooth is all ready to grow in its place. New teeth grow for the reptile's entire life. They're sharp and perfect for grabbing **prey**!

Crocodilians include crocodiles, alligators, and gharials.

Sticks and Stomps

FACT 5

Alligators and crocodiles do tricks with sticks!

Some alligators and crocodiles have learned a trick for when nearby water birds are building their nests. The clever predators pile sticks on their **snout**. When the birds fly down to get sticks—chomp—they become a quick snack.

Only crocodilians that live near water birds have learned to use this trick.

The wood turtle stomps for food.

When a wood turtle wants a worm dinner, it rocks back and forth, stomping its feet and shell on the ground. Worms underground feel the movement. They come to the surface. Snap! The wood turtle gobbles them up.

FACT 7

The alligator snapping turtle fishes with its tongue!

The tongue has a bright red tip that looks like a worm. The turtle stays still, opens its mouth, and moves its tongue, drawing a hungry fish to it. The fish swims up close. Snap! The turtle has its dinner.

A chameleon's tongue can pull in about half the reptile's body weight.

A chameleon's tongue is longer than its body!

When a chameleon sees a tasty bug, out shoots its long, speedy tongue. The end of the tongue is sticky and shaped like a club. Whoosh! The prey is caught, faster than you can blink an eye.

Beware!

FACT 9

About 100 types of lizards and 600 types of snakes are venomous.

The spitting cobra escapes predators by spitting **venom** into an enemy's eyes.

Many snakes and lizards have **developed** venom to keep predators away. They may spit it at an enemy or bite to let the venom out. The venom from a Komodo dragon bite is strong enough to kill its prey.

venomous snakes	venomous lizards
coral	Komodo dragon
copperhead	Gila monster
rattlesnake	Mexican beaded lizard
cottonmouth	bearded dragon
king cobra	common water monitor
green mamba	
tiger snake	
black mamba	
inland taipan	

Not every venomous reptile harms people, but it's important to be careful around these animals anyway!

FACT 10

Boa **constrictors** give their prey a deadly hug.

Boa constrictors can grow up to 13 feet (4 m) long. They wrap themselves around prey and hold on with their small, curved teeth. Then they squeeze tight, and the animal dies quickly. Pythons also kill prey this way.

Angry rattlesnakes make a lot of noise.

A rattlesnake rests quietly until it senses a predator nearby. Then it rises up, hisses, rattles its tail, and puffs up in warning. If the predator keeps coming, the rattlesnake strikes with its deadly bite and venom.

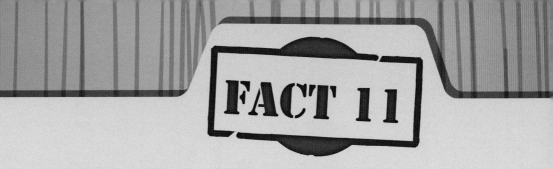

rattle

Scientists say rattlesnakes are the newest and most **evolved** snakes on Earth.

FACT 12

Snakes don't chew their food—they swallow prey whole!

A snake's prey may be larger than its body because a snake's **jaws** open very wide. Its skin **stretches**, and its bones move. Everything goes back into shape after the meal.

After a snake eats a large meal, it might not need to eat again for many days or even weeks!

The thorny devil lizard drinks from its own body!

This thirsty desert inhabitant lives in a very dry part of Australia. It's adapted by catching rain and dew between its scales and the spikes on its head and body. The water flows right into the lizard's mouth!

Now You See It, Now You Don't

FACT 14

Green mamba snakes look just like leaves in the trees where they live.

Some land reptiles use **camouflage** to hide! Greenish-brown tuataras can't be seen on the ground. Chameleons blend in so well they can hardly be seen at all!

Can the chameleon's camouflage trick you?

When looking up at this turtle's light underside, predators and prey might just think it's the sun shining through the water!

FACT 15

Green sea turtles are colored so they can't be seen from above or below in the water.

Green sea turtle shells are dark brown or green on top and lighter underneath their body. This makes it so the turtle is camouflaged whether another animal is looking up at it underwater or down at it from the sky.

The milk snake has developed its own costume over time.

The nonvenomous milk snake **mimics** the venomous coral snake. Both snakes have the same colors and are active at night. Predators stay away from the milk snake because they think it's a coral snake.

milk snake

coral snake

Here's a rhyme to help you tell the difference between a milk snake and coral snake:
If red touches black, he's your friend, Jack. If red touches yellow, he's a venomous fellow.

The satanic leaf-tailed gecko looks and acts like a dead leaf!

Using mimicry and camouflage, this bug-eating lizard fools its prey. Twisting its body, it hides under leaves until a bug comes along. Then it surprises its meal!

The satanic leaf-tailed gecko's camouflage can even make it look like a broken or old leaf breaking down!

FACT 18

The hognose snake plays dead to escape being eaten!

The hognose snake puffs up and flattens its head to look scary. It hisses loudly and pretends to strike. If these tricks don't work, the hognose snake rolls over, opens its mouth, and hangs out its tongue.

The hognose snake's body stays floppy even if a predator picks it up!

24

Many lizards can regrow a lost tail several times.

FACT 19

The tail of a gecko or a skink can break off and move around on the ground!

If the reptile is grabbed, their tail has special places where it breaks off. The confused predator watches the tail moving on the ground while the lizard runs to safety.

Many reptile babies use a special egg tooth to poke a hole in the shell when they're ready to come out of it.

Reptile eggs don't crack!

Reptiles lay their eggs on land. Some reptiles, like turtles, drop their eggs into deep holes. Their shells are leathery and don't break. The shell gives the reptiles more choices about where to make their nests.

The adult female reptile lays eggs.

Eggs develop.

The young reptile, or hatchling, leaves its egg.

Adult reptiles come together to make babies.

The young reptile grows slowly into an adult.

All reptiles have the same life cycle. Babies look like adults, but smaller.

Reptiles of All Sizes

Go anywhere in the world, except Antarctica, and you'll see reptiles. They come in all sizes, from the leaf chameleon, which is just over 1 inch (2.5 cm) long, to the reticulated python, which can be more than 30 feet (9.1 m) from end to end!

If you want to learn more about reptiles, visit a natural history museum or a zoo. Talk to a herpetologist. This is a person who studies reptiles. They'll know a lot about reptiles' amazing adaptations!

Komodo dragon

Herpetologists know how to handle many kinds of reptiles safely.

ancestor: an animal that comes before others in a family

behavior: the way an animal acts

camouflage: colors or shapes in animals that allow them to blend with their surroundings

constrictor: a snake that squeezes its prey to death

develop: the act or process of creating over time

environment: the weather, soil, and living things around something

evolved: to have grown and changed over time into a different state

jaws: the walls of the mouth

mimic: to copy

prey: an animal that is hunted by other animals for food

shed: to lose skin, hair, fur, or feathers naturally

slither: to slide easily over the ground

snout: the long nose of some animals

stretch: to grow larger

venom: something an animal makes in its body that can harm other animals

For More Information

Books

Brett, Flora. *A Reptile's View of the World*. Mankato, MN: Capstone Press, 2016.

McCarthy, Colin. *Reptile*. New York, NY: DK Publishing, 2012.

Websites

National Geographic Reptiles
animals.nationalgeographic.com/animals/reptiles/
Read all about reptiles, and watch videos of them in action.

San Diego Zoo Kids Reptiles
kids.sandiegozoo.org/animals/reptiles
Play games and watch videos as you learn cool facts about reptiles.

Smithsonian National Zoological Park: Reptiles and Amphibians
nationalzoo.si.edu/animals/reptilesamphibians/
Take a virtual visit to the Reptile Discovery Center at the National Zoo.